But the magic tree took no notice of his yelps. The badger would have to look after himself. It took him ages to free himself. He limped all the way home, rubbing his sore nose.

The young badger lived under the magic tree with all his family, mother father and lots of brothers and sisters. Can *you* see how many of them there are? When he was safely curled up in his burrow,

The MAGIC TREE and the CURIOUS BADGER

By Hannah E. Glease

Illustrated by Gillian Embleton

Scholastic Publications Ltd, in association with Pan Books Ltd

In deepest woodland stood an oak
That often smiled but never spoke

Upon its trunk so old and lined
It had a face for *you* to find

For no grown-up can ever see
The features of a magic tree

The animals and birds all knew
Exactly where this wise tree grew

They gathered in the leafy glade
And took protection from its shade

Two squirrels in its mouth had found
A safe dry home, well off the ground

And just above, beneath its brow
An owl perched on a bending bough

Some badgers burrowed underground
In tunnels spreading far around

And butterflies and birds and bees
Flew in from all the other trees

This story tells of a badger's fright
From the prickly ball he met one night

Only the moon and the magic tree could see the young badger as he nosed among a heap of leaves. Suddenly his snout hit something prickly and he was stuck. "Help, help," he squealed to the tree.

he told his younger brother all about the prickly ball.
"I'm not scared," said his brother as he drifted off to sleep. "Will you show me where it is tomorrow night?"

"I hope it won't stick to me," said the younger badger as they set off to find the ball. "Don't touch it, whatever you do," said the other, still nursing his sore paws. When they reached the leaves,

there was nothing to be seen. "The magic tree must have moved the nasty spiky thing," said the badger. The tree shook its head. It knew where the ball was and how it got there. Can *you* find it?

The badgers looked all night but they could not find the ball. The younger one grew tired and went back home. The older searched and searched until he was far away – too far away for the magic tree to look

after him. And the fox was on his trail. The badger did everything to fool the fox, so that he could not follow him. If *you* were the fox would you have known which trail to follow?

Next night, both badgers went to look again. The prickly ball was there, and so was the fox. "Let's see if he gets his nose stuck," said the badgers. But the fox did not have a chance to get stuck.

The magic tree made all the leaves blow about and when they settled, the ball was gone again. “Tomorrow night, we’ll watch the ball and find out how it disappears,” said the badgers.

When darkness fell the next night, the badgers were all ears and eyes. They heard a scuffling in the leaves and peered through the gloom. The prickly ball was moving! It was unrolling. Now the badgers

knew what the tree had known all along – the mysterious prickly ball was a hedgehog. It could run and walk, just like any of the other animals – when it wanted to.

Play and Learn

1 Ask questions to encourage the children to talk about the story in their own words. "Which animals do they like best and why? How did the badger feel when the fox was chasing him? How did he feel when he reached home?"

2 Together, make up a story about a hedgehog and a fox.

3 The hedgehog feels prickly. Ask the children to touch everyday objects and describe how they feel: rough, smooth, sticky, soft and so on.

4 Explain how the hedgehog curls up to protect itself from its enemies. Ask how other animals protect themselves from danger.

5 Ask the children to point out the badger's brothers and sisters and his father and mother.

6 Practice counting. Ask: "How many badgers are there in the burrow? How many would there be if one left the burrow?"

7 Talk about the colours in the pictures.

8 Point out the roots of the magic tree (pages 6 & 7). Explain how the tree sucks up its water through these roots. Rest a bulb on the rim of a jam jar half full of water and watch the roots grow.